Phone   4668

... to Boost Your
Communication Skills

Elizabeth Tierney

KOGAN
PAGE

First published in 1997
Reprinted 1997, 1998

Kogan Page Limited
120 Pentonville Road
London
N1 9JN

© Elizabeth P Tierney, 1997

The right of Elizabeth P Tierney to be identified as author of this work has been asserted by her in accordance with the Copyright, Designs and Patents Act 1988.

British Library Cataloguing in Publication Data
A CIP record for this book is available from the British Library.

ISBN 0 7494 2367 6

Typeset by Florencetype Ltd, Stoodleigh, Devon
Printed in England by Clays Ltd, St Ives plc

CONTENTS

The 30 Minutes Series

The Kogan Page 30 Minutes Series has been devised to give your confidence a boost when faced with tackling a new skill or challenge for the first time.

So the next time you're thrown in at the deep end and want to bring your skills up to scratch or pep up your career prospects, turn to the *30 Minutes Series* for help!

Titles available are:

30 Minutes Before Your Job Interview

30 Minutes Before a Meeting

30 Minutes Before a Presentation

30 Minutes to Boost Your Communication Skills

30 Minutes to Succeed in Business Writing

30 Minutes to Master the Internet

30 Minutes to Make the Right Decision

30 Minutes to Prepare a Job Application

30 Minutes to Write a Business Plan

30 Minutes to Write a Marketing Plan

30 Minutes to Write a Report

30 Minutes to Write Sales Letters

Available from all good booksellers.
For further information on the series, please contact:

Kogan Page, 120 Pentonville Road, London N1 9JN
Tel: 0171 278 0433 Fax: 0171 837 6348

INTRODUCTION

This book is designed to help you communicate more effectively. It is aimed in particular at business people who 1. recognise the important role communication plays in their organisations; 2. feel that the skills they currently possess can be improved; and 3. recognise how the realities of today's complex, global markets require effective communication skills.

As a business person, you interact with other people all the time. You meet, talk, fax, e-mail, write. But how *well* do you communicate? If you communicate well, ask yourself what are the benefits? If you are a less than excellent communicator, ask yourself instead: what are the costs of being an ineffectual communicator?

Good communicators are not always born; you can learn to be a good communicator. However, not all of us have the opportunity to be trained. Yet we should be, because many of the problems that occur in business stem from poor communication.

Although this book is designed to be read in a short time, it is intended to have long-term implications for you, your management abilities and effectiveness. It has implications for your organisations as well. The book consists of 15 sections, with questions to give you the opportunity to assess yourself. Every topic, every question is designed to boost your communication skills.

Good luck.

1

RECOGNISE THE BENEFITS OF BOOSTING YOUR COMMUNICATION SKILLS

Recognise that there are benefits to boosting your communication skills. 'What are they?' you may ask. Listen to these remarks. You've probably heard comments like them in your office:

Jim: 'I didn't know you wanted me to interview the internal applicants as well as the external ones!'

Jane: 'Sorry. I didn't realise that you needed the data for last night's client meeting.'

Harry: 'I would have arranged the seating in the conference room, but nobody told me that it needed to be changed.'

Amy: 'Interesting presentation. But what was the point of it?'

Have you heard remarks like these? Have you ever said them? Now the harder question: have similar comments ever been made about you? Or to you? Let's hope not. What you have just read is a list of communication failures. And when communication fails, business is affected.

When communication fails

Let's examine each of those comments more closely to determine what might have prompted them.

Jim has mishandled some candidates for a job because he didn't know who he was to interview. **Communication failure.**

Jane is apologising for failing to provide essential information on time for a meeting. **Communication failure.**

Harry is justifying why he didn't do what he was supposed to have done. **Communication failure.**

Amy is bewildered by what she heard. **Communication failure.**

While each issue is different, there is a common thread: each remark is an illustration of **communication failure**. True, the comments are taken out of context, but we can still surmise that they are being said because:

- Something was not said that should have been said;
- Something was assumed that should not have been assumed;
- Something was unclear that should have been made clear.

As a consequence, communication has failed for Jim, Jane and the others. Communication has also failed for the people who believed that they had effectively shared essential information with them.

What are the implications of failed communication?

Pretend that Jim, Harry, Amy and Jane report to you. Make an even more difficult assumption: that they are talking about you. How might each of the following scenarios affect you as a manager or your organisation? What do you think are the implications in each case?

- A member of your staff mishandled an interview involving internal job applicants;

- A member of your staff didn't have essential data ready on time for a client meeting;

- A member of your staff didn't arrange the conference room. At the last minute you have to move tables and chairs;

- A member of your staff didn't understand the point of a talk that you gave.

Horrible as the consequences may be, imagine that all these scenarios occurred within a day or two. Think about the costs you or your organisation might incur. Did you note any of these?

- Loss of time
- Loss of respect
- Loss of business
- Loss of money
- Loss of confidence

- Loss of credibility
- Loss of relationships
- Loss of staff
- Loss of trust
- Loss of a client

Any or all of these could have serious consequences for you or your business. The damage increases with additional costs. As already suggested, the comments reflect miscommunication. The seeds of those communication failures were sown in the preceding days, weeks or minutes. Messages that should have been transmitted clearly to Jim, Harry and Jane and the others were not. As a consequence, they didn't do what they were supposed to do. When communication fails, managers and organisations are affected.

When communication succeeds

This time assume that communication has succeeded: Jim interviewed all the appropriate candidates; Jane supplied the data that you need for the client on time; Harry pre-arranged the chairs and tables; Amy recognised the point of your talk.

Again, assume Jim and the others work for you. However, instead of listing losses, what are some benefits that accrue to you or your organisation because of successful communication?

Do your answers look like these?

- People feel good
- People do their jobs well
- People work together
- People feel motivated

- People understand
- People save time
- People feel empowered
- People assume responsibility
- People share information
- People respect, trust and like you
- People listen.

By reviewing your own answers, can you see how you benefit from boosting your communication? Poor communication leads to negative outcomes. Effective communication leads to positive ones.

Summary

The ability to communicate well is an important aspect of your management style and skills, and one that is frequently overlooked. Many people assume that we all have good communication skills, but the truth is that we don't.

By recognising the importance of boosting your communication skills

- You motivate, explain or convince
- You save time – your own and that of others
- You encourage a sense of organisation or teamwork
- You reinforce your professionalism
- You develop and maintain relationships, not only within the organisation but outside it as well
- You are credible and trusted
- You are liked
- You empower people
- You are heard.

UNDERSTAND THE COMMUNICATION PROCESS

The communication process is both subtle and complex. By examining the process in steps, you are better able to see how and why mis-communication may occur. Thus you can anticipate and prevent communication breakdowns.

Three important terms

The communication process occurs in seven steps. Let's begin our discussion by referring to three terms: **message**; **sender**; and **receiver**.

- The **message** is the idea, thought or feeling to be shared

- The **sender** is the person who communicates the message

- The **receiver** is the person or audience for whom the communication is intended.

Assuming that you are the sender, let's look at each of the seven steps:

Step 1: Have a message

You have an idea, a thought or a feeling you want to share with someone else. This is a **message**. Messages range from simple greetings like 'Hello' to complex ones like feasibility studies or political speeches. Examples of simple messages might be your wanting John to phone you, or your hoping that Sue will accompany you to a conference. Convincing a customer that a particular product will make life better or easier, or wanting to share innovative notions with your boss might involve more complex messages.

Step 2: Choose between words, actions and images

You have decided what message you want to convey. Next you must decide how best to capture the essence of that message. Should it be in words? Would your ideas be received better if you made hand gestures instead? Would designing and sending a picture, map or graph explain your ideas more clearly?

Suppose you wanted John to phone you. What options do you have?

- Did you indicate that you would talk or write to John?
- Would you have signalled him with your hands?
- Would you have drawn a picture of stick figures holding telephones?

Similar options are available when you indicate to Sue that you want her to accompany you to the conference. Ditto when you develop an advertising campaign or want to share your innovative ideas with your supervisor. You, the **sender**, determine the best method for communicating the **message**.

Not only do you decide between using words, actions or images, you must also determine **which** words, actions or images to use. If you and John are French, you may choose to write a note in French. However, if you and John are Japanese, German, Italian or South African, French might not be the wisest choice of language.

Step 3: Send the message

There are several options. Suppose you chose words for your message to John. How might you get those words to him?

- Did you put written words on a note and leave them on John's desk?

- Did you ask a colleague to give John the message for you?

- Did you phone John and leave your message on his answer phone?

- Did you write the message and send it via e-mail or fax?

- If you chose images instead of words, did you signal to John across the office by holding your closed hand to your ear like a telephone?

Step 4: Receive the message

Until now, you, **the sender**, have been making all the decisions. However, once you send the message, the control shifts to the **receiver** or **receivers**. If John is going to know you want him to phone you, **he** needs to receive your message. For Sue to accompany you to the conference, **she** has to receive the message. For consumers to test your product, **they** have to receive your message. For the boss to consider your recommendation, **he** or **she** has to get the message, too.

Step 5: Interpret the message

It's a good day. John, Sue, the consumer and your boss actually received the messages that you sent them. Hopefully, they will interpret your message as you meant it to be. In other words:

- If you wrote a note in English, the receiver must interpret the writing and the choice of words;
- If you left a verbal message, the receiver has to interpret the sounds;
- If you designed a print ad campaign, the receiver has to interpret the copy and the visuals;
- If you chose to gesture, the receiver has to interpret your movements.

Step 6: Act on the message

We said that it was a good day. John got your note. Sue received your phone call. The consumer saw your ad, and your boss' read your memo. Remember, the receivers are in control. At this point, you can only hope that your initial choices were wise ones and that the receivers will do what you want them to do. At this point, you don't know.

What might happen to the message to your boss? Will the boss put your memo in a file, unread? In the bottom of the in-tray? In the bin? Will you be called into the office for a chat? For a reprimand? For overstepping your bounds? Will you be praised for your initiative?

Step 7: Provide feedback

Feedback is vital because it provides you with information about how your message was received and interpreted. Once you have it, you can plan your next message. What kind of feedback might you get from the messages that you sent?

- John will phone you back, or he won't
- Sue will tell you that she is looking forward to the conference or she will cry off
- The boss will want to discuss your ideas or not
- The consumer will buy your product or not, or there may be no feedback.

Now you are no longer the sender; you are the recipient of someone else's message. So, the cycle begins again with someone else having a message to send to you, to which you will respond or not.

Summary

To boost your communication skills, it is vital to understand what you are doing when you communicate. That way you can anticipate possible breakdowns. Think about the seven steps in the process.

3

REFLECT ON
WHAT HINDERS
COMMUNICATION

Now that we have examined the seven steps in the communication process, let us see how that process can break down or be blocked.

Major blockages to communication

The message itself

Messages are often incomplete. Why? The senders don't thoroughly think through the ideas they want to share with others and the ideas therefore remain vague or confusing. Receivers like Amy are left wondering about the point of a particular presentation. Poorly thought out messages may result in weak or unclear memos, reports, e-mails, faxes, interviews, chats, advertisements, annual reports or contracts. Poorly thought out or confusing messages prevent effective communication.

Inappropriate choice of words, actions or images

Suppose the sender uses words to describe the construction of a building when a picture or an architectural drawing would have been more meaningful. Perhaps the sender chose to draw a picture to teach you how to drive a car when actions would have been clearer.

Also, the decision to use words, actions or images may have been appropriate, but the selection of the particular words, actions or images may have been inappropriate. Geographical regions have their own phrases or patterns of usage and people from outside that region may not understand because they are unfamiliar with the local idiom. In other words, communication can be blocked by the sender making inappropriate choices of words, actions or images.

Failure to transmit the message

Even when a message is well thought out and appropriate words, actions or images are selected, the transmission of a message can fail:

- The fax machine runs out of paper
- A letter is put on the wrong desk
- Someone forgets to deliver a phone message
- The computer system is down
- Your voice-mailbox may be full
- Telephones – cellular or otherwise – may be ringing while you are talking

- Planes take off or fly overhead
- Construction is in progress next door.

However, communication may also be prevented because the method of transmission was inappropriate. We may have chosen to write a letter and send it in the post when a fax would have been wiser. Perhaps an e-mail might have been better than the fax. In a given situation a telephone call might have been more appropriate than a memo. Perhaps a one-page report might have been better than a casual chat or a 30-page document.

Failure to receive the message

Sometimes the receiver simply doesn't get the message. Remember Jim and his colleagues?

- Maybe Jim didn't hear that you wanted all the internal candidates interviewed
- Harry didn't get your message about arranging the chairs in the conference room
- Did Jane skim a lengthy memo and miss the part that indicated when you needed the data for the client meeting?
- Amy may not have understood the talk because the concepts were poorly thought out or badly presented. Maybe she was confused by the use of technical language. Maybe she couldn't decipher the complex visuals.

Then again, maybe they didn't get the message because they were preoccupied: thinking, worrying or concentrating on other matters, personal or professional. We are well aware that stress affects clear thinking. Deadlines, bills, family pressures, pending meetings, or important holidays create stress and may block communication.

Misinterpreting the message

If, for example, you use the language of marketing with a group of non-marketers not everyone will understand your use of terms like niches, market share, product placement and life cycles. Or, if you use techno-speak with non-technical people, not everyone will follow your meaning. Thus they may miss or misinterpret the message.

However, personality and perception alter messages as well. Maybe your message was well thought out, but Amy didn't get the point of the presentation because she didn't like you personally. She may have failed to get the message because she had her own perceptions about your motivations for giving the talk. She may still be harbouring a grudge about a denied request. In other words, communication may be blocked by the receiver's knowledge or attitudes.

Besides these major blockages, in your experience what else has hindered communication?

Summary

Communication is frequently prevented because of major blockages.

■ The message itself is confused or unclear

■ The choice of words, actions or images is inappropriate

■ The transmission has failed

■ The receiver has not got the message

■ The receiver has misinterpreted your message.

Let's be proactive now, and examine how to improve the odds of your communicating effectively.

4

DO YOUR HOMEWORK

By thinking through the communication process and recognising where most breakdowns occur for you, you can anticipate problems and prepare for them.

True, we cannot plan for everything. We all call or attend spontaneous meetings, engage in casual chats or give impromptu talks. However, more often than not, we can plan ahead and do our homework. Doing so increases the odds of communications being more successful.

As you reflect on past situations, you may notice that your communication problems recur in similar situations. What can you do to avoid this?

Set aside time to do your homework

Spend time thinking through a situation rather than acting immediately. While it is important to note times of meetings, appointments and flights in your diary or organiser, you should also set aside time for thinking, asking questions, planning, drafting, practising or editing. During these times, you should be uninterrupted – no phone calls, no visitors.

All too often we give talks off the cuff, submit rough drafts as final documents and conduct meetings without planning for them. Try to avoid this kind of impromptu communication. Instead, make time to do your homework. But what should you be doing with that time?

Think

You should analyse the situation in which the communication is going to occur. Is it an interview? A new client meeting? Are you talking or listening to a difficult or unhappy customer? Are you meeting with a disgruntled employee? Are you submitting a memo or report? Are you writing up a meeting? Do you have to give a talk? Answer questions? Address a conference? Don't just take action. Think first.

Would other people describe you as someone who acts first and then thinks or as one who thinks first and then acts?

Ask questions

You should direct questions to yourself as well as to others. Use the old standards: who? what? why? when? where? how? If you ask and then answer these questions in advance, you will anticipate problems and identify opportunities. We will examine the implications of some of the questions in a few minutes.

Plan

Once you have answers to your questions, you should be planning: determining what message(s) you want to send and how you are going to send them. You should be planning as much of your communication as possible: your talks, your agendas, your interview questions or answers. You should outline your thoughts and list your priorities.

Draft your ideas

Most formal communication involves words of some kind: memos; letters; faxes; status reports; talks; interviews; presentations; questions and answers. Being an effective communicator isn't about staying up all night to hand in a final report the next day. Effective communication is about getting your rough thoughts down on paper, on the computer or on a tape, and then taking the time to critically review your work before you distribute the final version.

Practise your oral communication

If your communication involves giving a talk, making a presentation, or giving a progress or status report at a meeting, you should practise aloud what you intend to say.

Edit your written communication and check your visuals

Editing involves reading what you have written to ensure that the words you have chosen clearly and accurately convey what you intend to share with the readers. Checking your visuals means ensuring that the audience can see and interpret any images, graphs or tables you have prepared.

Summary

Too often what should still be a rough draft is submitted as final. Too often a talk is not rehearsed enough. You should set aside time to: think; ask questions; plan; draft your thoughts; practise your oral communication; edit your written communication and check your visuals.

Now let's take a longer look at the message itself.

5

KNOW YOUR MESSAGE AND YOUR PURPOSE

Surprisingly, one of the most difficult aspects of communicating is determining the message and its purpose. Often, we haven't set aside the time to do our homework, so our messages are not as clear and focused as they could be. To ensure that our messages are accurate and precisely targeted, we have to ask questions. If we don't, we risk sending messages that say too much or too little. We may wander off at tangents. We may include notions that distract from our original point or don't move our arguments along. As a result, we may give talks that result in feedback like Amy's. We may write reports that are convoluted, that people are reluctant to read.

Think of a typical morning at work. What are some of the different reasons you have for communicating your ideas or feelings to your colleagues? To inform? To convince? To entertain? To motivate? To sell? To share good news? To deliver bad news? To dissuade? To discourage? To deny? Any others?

We may use different words, but for the most part we persuade. Motivating is persuading. We are persuading when we make remarks like:

'We are an excellent company to work for.'

'I am an ideal candidate.'

'Taking this approach might be easier.'

'This method might work.'

'This system doesn't address the problem.'

'You should change your methods.'

At this point, you might well say: 'I know what I want to communicate'.You may. But more often than not, as we have said, concepts have not been as carefully thought through as they might have been, often because of time restraints.

Refine your message

Because avoiding confusion is crucial and time is precious, here is a simple, quick technique for refining your message. Suppose the general theme of your message is:

A policy

To refine the theme initially, ask questions like: Which policy? Government? Military? Industrial, industry-wide? Educational? If you don't want to discuss **a policy**, narrow your thinking to:

A human resource policy

Now you might ask yourself: Which human resource policy? All policies in general? In our country? Throughout the world ? Is it a policy relating to this organisation? Is it a current policy or one dating back 20 years? Is it a policy in our division? If you know that you don't want to discuss **a human resource policy**, narrow your message to:

A human resource policy in our organisation

Now you might ask: What if you have more than one human resource policy? If you do, you might narrow your topic further to:

Our company's policy on performance appraisal

Continue asking questions. Perhaps ask yourself if this is a new policy or an old one. Narrow your message again:

Our company's current policy on performance appraisal

Now ask: Do you want to discuss the policy? Or do you want to discuss the actual appraisal document? Perhaps you want to discuss the method of using the appraisal? You are narrowing your topic once again:

Our company's current performance appraisal document

But what aspect of the current performance appraisal document do you want to address? Was the document changed? Do the changes matter? Do the reasons for the change matter? Is the document in use? Is it under review? Is it being tested? Are you scrapping the document? Your answers will enable you to refine your message again:

The importance of understanding the reasons for the changes in our company's current performance appraisal document

We could go on *ad infinitum*, but let's stop here. You may ultimately decide to lead a discussion about the time required to complete the document. Perhaps you will decide to write and distribute a memo about the importance of clarifying certain language in the document. Maybe you will draft some guidelines about the implications of the changes in the document.

What is important is that you have refined your thinking. You have narrowed the topic.

Be sure to ask why

But wait. Be sure to ask **why** you want to communicate the reasons for the changes in the current performance appraisal document and **why** what you are communicating is essential for the audience.

One way to determine if your purpose is clear is to ask yourself questions like: 'So what?' 'What is the point?' 'Why does the audience need to know this information?' 'What difference does the message make to them?' The answers will remind you if there is some aspect of the previous document that was not useful or was problematic. Are the changes going to affect promotion or retention? Will the changes take more time? Less time? In other words, what's the point of sharing the communication?

Yes, I am labouring the point. But consider the memos and reports you have read and have had to reread. Recall the talks you have heard or the meetings that you have attended. Think about the time that was wasted because what you were hearing or seeing was confusing. Often we think we have thought through our ideas thoroughly when we haven't. Looking at the example above, we knew that we should discuss 'a policy' but without carefully refining our ideas, we could have started by discussing policies in general and meandered along until we eventually got to the point. In the meantime, the audience is wandering too. They may resent the time that you are wasting.

Now *you* try it. Select a topic, then narrow it. Any topic will do: football; new product development; promotion; advertising campaign; misuse of company time; staffing; budget; the company outing.

Seek additional input

What you just did, you did on your own. Sometimes, however, you need other people's assistance to clarify your purpose. That is true particularly when someone else has asked you to undertake the work. Your boss may have wanted you to submit a report or an update for a meeting. In such instances you may have to ask your boss a few questions. The answers should help you to decide what should be included or excluded and why those exclusions, inclusions or emphases should be there.

The process of refining your message and determining your purpose only takes a few minutes and it is time well spent to ensure that your audience will get your point. You will also save time by not having to repeatedly clarify and explain.

Summary

Many messages are unclear. They often include too much or too little. Therefore, be sure that you know the purpose of your message. For your message to be clear to your audience, you, the sender, should:

- Refine your message by asking questions of yourself and of others
- Ask yourself why the audience needs to get the message or how will they benefit from the communication.

6

ANALYSE YOUR AUDIENCE

Analysing the audience requires only a few minutes. When you sought to refine the message, you may have asked others and you may want to do this again in order to learn about the audience. Your objective is to know as much as possible about the person or persons with whom you are going to be interacting in a meeting, an interview, on the phone, via fax, at a conference (or even waiting in the conference room). Why?

Having information about the audience enables you to tailor your thoughts to ensure that your message is received as accurately as possible. Knowledge of the audience increases the odds of your message being received as it was intended.

Ask questions

With how many people will you be interacting?

Will it be one to one? Will there be three on a telephone conference call? Will there be ten around a boardroom table? Will there be 20 in a staff meeting or 350 in an annual meeting? How many people are going to read your report or memo?

This will help you determine the degree of interaction, formality or informality required by the situation. It may affect the length of a talk, meeting or document, or influence the type of information you include.

To whom will your ideas be distributed?

Who else, apart from your specific intended audience, might also be privy to what you have communicated? Will a copy of what you have written be made public or reach the desk of the managing director or a client?

Knowing the answer may affect what confidential information you include or what points to emphasise or downplay.

Who are the people in the audience ?

What are their names? What are their job titles? What are their responsibilities? What are their departments? What are their specialisations? Are they union representatives, clients, customers, board members, auditors, competitors, colleagues, lawyers or bankers? Are you talking to a brand manager or a shop steward about a marketing issue?

Knowing the answer may affect the background information you include or exclude. You don't want to tell people what they already know, or refrain from telling them what they need to know.

What is the audience's relationship with you and with each other?

Have you previously met your audience? Are they strangers to you and unfamiliar with the organisation? Are they people with whom you hope to have a long-term relationship? Is the relationship one of supervisor/subordinate? Is the relationship strained because of a history of problems between you and the audience? Are you dealing with a difficult employee or an unhappy customer? Will they be responsive?

Knowing the answer may influence what you include or exclude and what tone you use.

What does the audience already know about what you want to communicate?

Is your report the outcome of a previous discussion? Are you raising new issues in a talk? What does the audience know or understand about the subject? Have you shared these ideas with them before? Does the message include language or images that are unfamiliar to them? What background do you have to provide?

Knowing the answer will prevent you from boring people by telling them what they already know or confusing them by excluding essential information.

What demographic information is available to you about the audience?

In other words, what is the gender, nationality and/or age of the members of the audience?

This will help you to determine if there are words or images you should exclude because they will not be meaningful. For instance, nationality, gender and age might affect your choice of analogies or examples. International news is available, but a particular local or regional event may hold no meaning for the audience. Avoid discussing past events if the audience is too young to understand their significance. An analogy designed for a 20-year-old Englishman may not be understood by an 80-year-old Japanese woman.

What are the politics?

What is the decision-making process? Which individuals have influence over others? Is your message controversial? Who is jockeying for position?

Knowing the answer will assist you in making choices which take into account biases, sensitivities and/or prejudices.

What are the unique personality traits you might have to deal with?

People are unique individuals. With whom precisely are you sharing your ideas? Who is reflective? Who is belligerent? Who needs attention? Who pays attention to detail? Who shoots from the hip, and who plays it safe in a public forum?

Understanding the personalities involved may affect your choice of style, tone, content or approach or assist you in preparing for questions.

Is your message confidential?

What is your audience allowed to know without violating confidentiality?

This will help you to determine what you can and cannot include.

In terms of the nature of the audience what is the biggest challenge that you face in delivering your message?

Summary

To complete your analysis of the audience take some time to ask questions, which should enable you to learn as much as possible about the individuals and their relationships with you.

7

DETERMINE HOW TO COMMUNICATE YOUR MESSAGE

Consider what you have achieved so far. You have thought through what you want to communicate and why, who will be the recipient of your message and what you should do to be clear. At this point it is a good idea to take another few minutes to decide **how** you want to share your ideas or feelings. In other words, you should decide whether to write a memo, meet in your office, have a casual chat in the corridor or choose another option.

Evaluate your choices

Earlier we suggested that you could opt for words, actions or images. What is important is understanding the range of choices that you can make, and the advantages and disadvantages of each. You want to select the most appropriate forms for the particular messages that you want to send. Before looking at some of the differences, consider your choices.

Which methods of communication do you use most often? Telephone? Informal chat? Lecture? Formal meetings? E-mail? Formal reports? Informal reports? Memos? Fax? Mail? Note? Photographs? Spreadsheets? Sketches, blueprints? Hand gestures? Cartoons? X-rays? What else?

Circumstances may determine the most appropriate method. When you decide how to disseminate your message, consider the implications of your choice. Considering the topic, is it best that you present a formal talk? Would the topic be better handled in small groups? In one-to-one meetings? Should the topic be handled in a quick one-page memo to all concerned? Or would a 30- or 40-page document be better? Does the urgency require that you send your message over the phone or via e-mail? Would you prefer that people have time to think? Then you would need to distribute something to be read before discussion.

Consider the implications

Ask yourself questions about such issues as the size and nature of the audience, formality, urgency, emphasis or confidentiality.

■ Do you want to have a record of your communication or not?

■ Do you want your message to be received quickly or slowly?

■ Do you want the audience to have the opportunity to reflect on what you have communicated, or to give you an immediate response?

- Do you want to see or hear the immediate feedback or not?

- Do you want your message to be formal or informal?

- Do you want your message to be backed up with data or not?

- Do you want to be able to distribute the same message to a large number of people?

- Is there a danger that what you have communicated will be used inappropriately?

- Do you want to be able to spontaneously modify your message?

- Do you want to be able to react to feedback immediately?

Summary

Determine how to communicate your message. Not only should you consider what you are sharing and why you are sharing it, it is equally important to consider *how* you want to convey the message.

Different methods have different implications. Therefore, it is important that you weigh such issues as formality, the nature and size of the audience, urgency, emphasis and confidentiality when you determine how you are going to say, write or do whatever you are going to communicate.

By this point, you should know what you are going to communicate, to whom and how. Now take some time to impose structure on your ideas.

8

ORGANISE YOUR THOUGHTS

The most effective messages are well-organised. Consider these points:

- Establish the context
- Include only the essentials
- Create a basic structure.

Establish the context

This means bringing the audience into the picture, or providing the background for what is to follow. Let us use as an example the openings of television shows and films. The audience is often brought into the story by the use of a long shot: we see a picture of a city on the horizon, then the camera zooms in on a particular area of that city. Often we are shown a distinctive landmark. Finally, the camera homes in on one building, one window then one room, where we meet the characters. In seconds, the context is established.

Apply the same principle if you are speaking or writing. The audience should be brought into the picture. Earlier, we made the point that communication may be hindered by the audience's preoccupations. You will improve the odds of their following your train of thought if you give them sufficient information to establish some background for what you intend to discuss.

How might you establish the context if you were asked to speak or write about each of three items? Suppose the topic is the plan for the redesign of the conference room. You might introduce this by discussing the importance of the conference room or the history of the conference room or the problems with the conference room, before going on to discuss the nature of the redesign.

What background might you give in a discussion of each of the following?

(a) At a staff meeting, how might you explain why the company is changing its logo?

(b) What background might you provide to explain the follow-up activities from a previous meeting?

(c) What information might you include to introduce your recommendations to a new client?

Include only the essentials

Hone and refine your material and exclude what is extraneous.

For example, in a half-hour interview, if you spend too much time discussing the weather, you may not get around to asking the essential questions designed to determine whether or not you are meeting a viable candidate for a position in your organisation. The same is true of the candidate who provides lengthy answers. Instead of making three or four important points about his or her credentials and suitability for the position, the candidate will have used up the time on non-essentials.

This is also true of a report. You can spend 15 pages waxing philosophical about a non-essential issue. In a talk, you can waste precious minutes telling interesting stories instead of clarifying your points. The same is true of a conversation, a counselling session, a memo or a report. It is important to stay focused on the message and eliminate the extraneous. Sometimes the part that people remember is the story, joke or anecdote, not your key points.

Create a basic structure

Most of us remember information more easily when it has some kind of structure. Books, plays or games typically have a basic structure: the beginning, the middle and the end. The beginning or introduction, explains what you are going to do or say. The middle, the explanation or exposition, develops the points or arguments you have introduced. The end, the conclusion, is a restatement or reminder to your audience of what you said in the beginning.

This book has a structure. The introduction indicated there would be 15 sections. Having read that at the outset, you expect 15. If only seven appear, you have been misled and may feel confused. You may actually check back to verify what you read.

Audiences in general are more comfortable and better able to follow your thinking if you create a structure. Letters, memos, short reports, long reports, talks all have a structure: beginning, middle and end. A long report may be structured differently and contain not only an introduction but also procedures, findings, conclusions and recommendations. Whether the report is five or 100 pages long, the material should be organised in a similar fashion.

This is also true of a meeting. An agenda provides a structure and orders the meeting. First on the agenda may be the presentation of old business, which means you go over anything that was unresolved at the previous meeting. Your agenda will also have a list of new items. The order of the list usually dictates the order of discussion. The final item may be called new business and typically refers to items that have never been discussed at meetings before.

Having a statement at the beginning which explains your purpose makes an effective opening. At the end you should restate it to help the audience remember your initial message.

Summary

Organise your ideas to assist your audience in following your thinking. To begin the process:

- Establish the context
- Include only the essentials
- Create a structure.

Once you have a basic structure, sequence the information to ensure that the audience can follow your logic and retain the information.

SEQUENCE
INFORMATION

To assist your reader or listener in following your logic or your argument, there is more organising that you can do. You can sequence your information.

Sequencing creates order for your information or for your arguments. Think about car licence numbers or telephone numbers. Most of us find it easier to remember numbers that have some sort of logic or sequence. This is demonstrated when we create our own access codes: because it is easier to recall patterns of letters or numbers, we create codes that are names or a meaningful set of numbers like birthdays or anniversaries.

In order to sequence effectively, look through your material to decide how best to order the points you intend to make to support your arguments. The following are some methods for sequencing information. They can be used for either the written or spoken word.

Chronology

A chronological approach is one in which you sequence information or data in terms of time. For example, you might start in the present and work back to the past or vice versa rather than randomly referring to something that happened last Tuesday, then the previous Friday, then today and then Tuesday again.

Numerical or alphabetical order

This involves sequencing information by using numbers or the alphabet. This book contains 15 sections: the first is one, the second is two, and so on. In a meeting you may wish to indicate that you have three reasons for supporting a particular position, so you discuss one, then two and then three. You may give your boss a memo with five recommendations for team-building. Each recommendation is numbered and you should refer to each of the numbers as you develop your message. You can also choose to use letters of the alphabet.

Theory to practice

When you present the concept first, followed by an explanation of how the concept is used in practice, you are sequencing from theory to application or practice. Suppose you are speaking or writing about your strategic plan. You might begin by discussing the plan from a theoretical perspective and continue by describing how the plan would be put into practice.

Order of importance

Another method is to arrange your data in order of importance. Frequently, this approach is coupled with numbering.

Because people tend to remember beginnings and ends, you might decide to place your strongest argument first or possibly last. Depending on where you put your strongest arguments, the other points would follow. We tend to bury our weakest arguments in the middle. In other words, you determine what order is most appropriate for the audience and the situation.

Spatial order

Yet another method is to sort information in space: that is, you discuss your topic in terms of its spatial relationships. You may use left to right or right to left. You may use north to south or south to north. You may go from back to front or front to back. You may go from side to side or top to bottom. Suppose your firm has branch offices. Wanting to show them on the map, you point first to the east and then to the west or from north to south. When using a chart or graph, you may want to have the readers or listeners look at the left side first before asking them to look to the right. For most of us, it is easier to visualise spatial relationships when we are presented with a clear sequence of ideas or images.

Mnemonics

A mnemonic is a memory aid. Thus, another method of ordering information is to create a word or device that captures the essence of your message and also orders your information. It may be a combination of letters that reflect your key points. For example, you have five points to make. The first is about **P**eople; the second is about the **O**rganisation; the third is about **W**ork; the fourth is about **E**nergy; and the fifth is about **R**espect. These five letters spell out the word **POWER**. The audience should be aided in remembering your points by your using the word **POWER** and clearly explaining what each of the letters means. But be careful that your mnemonic is not more memorable than your message.

Whether you choose one or another of these techniques or combine them, what is vital is that you create an internal sequence. This will enable your audience to follow your logic much more readily. In a sense Web sites follow that principle. The typical Web site has a home page or main message with several key points. Each point may be a link. Each link may then have another five.

Think about the last report you wrote or presentation you gave. If you sequenced information, what approach did you use? If you didn't sequence information, in retrospect, which of the preceding approaches might have been appropriate for the topic?

Summary

When you have established a beginning, middle and end, you should sequence your reasons or arguments. When you do, you help the audience to follow your thinking by creating a more memorable order. Some methods for sequencing information are:

- Chronology
- Numerical or alphabetical order
- Theory to practice
- Order of importance
- Spatial order
- Mnemonics.

You have designed your message. Now you need to think about the manner in which you are going to express it.

10

DETERMINE THE APPROPRIATE TONE

You have heard people say, 'Don't take that tone with me'. We understand tone of voice when we speak, but writing has a tone as well. Choice of tone impacts your message however you communicate it.

If you make an inappropriate choice:

- You can lose an audience by offending them;
- You can lose an audience by patronising them;
- You can lose your audience by demeaning them;
- You can lose your audience by insulting them;
- You can lose your audience by frightening them.

However, if you make an appropriate choice:

- You can win your audience by empowering them;
- You can win your audience by listening to them;
- You can win your audience by respecting their intelligence and knowledge;

- You can win your audience by recognising individual worth;
- You can win your audience with warmth and charm.

Tone has to do with speaking or writing in a way that is appropriate for a particular audience, a particular issue and a particular situation. Tone is determined by your word choices, by your sentence choices, by intonation, by your demeanour, by your facial expression and by your voice.

Imagine that you have been invited to speak at a wedding reception. Most likely you would be lighthearted and entertaining. If you stepped to the head table, appeared sombre-faced and lectured the newly married couple in eight- and nine-syllable words or read lengthy passages from Milton, you would startle the audience. Not that there is anything wrong with Milton, but given the setting that approach might be disconcerting.

Imagine landing at an international airport. You are greeted by a customs agent who hugs you and smiles, offers you a warm welcome and then tells a joke. Then you are informed that you are suspected of having entered the country illegally and that you will be departing on the next plane. Confused? Both of these are an extreme illustrations, but you can see that tone can be misleading.

Your behaviour

Your facial expression, your stance and your posture as well as your tone of voice all affect your message and your receiver. Consider whether or not to smile or frown. Should you shout or whisper your message? Are you seated while the receiver stands? Do you gesture and point?

Whether you are running a business meeting, answering the phone or writing a report, you should decide how formal or informal to be. In a meeting, tone might be determined by how you sit and by how you proceed through an agenda. Do you sit on the edge of the desk with jacket off, shoes dangling from your toes and ask, 'What's up?' Do you have prearranged seating around a boardroom table? Are you wearing your jacket? Is it buttoned? Do you open the meeting and move systematically through a pre-written agenda?

In interviews, you decide what image or tone you want to set for the interviewee if you are the interviewer. If you are the interviewee, you also set the tone. You decide whether this is a time for frivolity or for earnest behaviour.

Your word choices

Writers or speakers can patronise the audience with their word choices: when words like 'clearly', 'obviously' or 'of course' are used, this may suggest to the audience that they should know all about the subject already. Words like these suggest that the sender feels it is a waste of time explaining it to you. To patronise an audience is to insult them.

The same is true of written work. Do you adopt casual language? Do you use slang, or more formal language?

Suppose that you are announcing the closure of a plant and the lay-off of 30 of your staff. Suppose you were announcing a year-end bonus. How might you alter your tone in each situation?

Summary

You can insult, frighten or offend with an inappropriate tone, or show your respect for the audience by selecting the appropriate one. Consider your behaviour and your word choices. We've already mentioned the importance of selecting your words carefully, but there are other reasons to do so besides establishing the tone of your message.

SELECT WORDS, ACTIONS AND IMAGES WITH CARE

Now it is time to focus on the words, actions and images that you plan to use. Choosing the right ones can enhance your communication, which is the purpose of this tip. The following are some suggestions for selecting appropriate words, actions and images:

- Avoid hyperbole
- Avoid qualifiers
- Keep your communication simple
- Be consistent
- Be specific
- Use appropriate images: verbal or physical
- Consider confidentiality
- Be sensitive to inadvertent insults.

Avoid hyperbole

Whether you speak or write, there is often a temptation to exaggerate or to overgeneralise. We might inadvertently refer to 'all of our clients' when we actually only mean 12 of the 20. We may say 'everybody' when we really mean 'most people'. It is important, therefore, to double check when you run through or edit your work to be sure that you have not exaggerated but are accurate. Your credibility is at stake if one reader or listener hears a comment to the effect that we 'always' do something when, in fact, the company doesn't 'always'. If the company does something 'most of the time', then say so.

Avoid qualifiers

Qualifiers are little words and phrases like 'sort of, 'kind of', or 'rather'. We tend to use them when we can't find the right word. We might find ourselves in a sticky situation and say that we have 'sort of a problem' or a 'bit of a problem'. The audience might ask or think, 'What sort of a problem?' It might be a catastrophe, a mishap, a concern, a dilemma, or a disaster. What does 'sort of' mean? As writers or speakers we should spend time selecting the words that reflect what we mean instead of resorting to waffle.

Keep your communication simple

Avoid sentences that go on for paragraphs; avoid paragraphs that go on for pages; and avoid using complex or unusual words when simple or familiar ones will do. Do we have to live in abodes instead of houses? Must we interface and liaise? Instead, can't we meet and talk?

Keeping it simple also means avoiding jargon and technical language. As we said, jargon may only be understood by members of a certain trade or industry. There is no problem with jargon or technical language if you are sure all members of the audience know the meaning of the terms or phrases or can translate what you are communicating. If they don't or can't, they will not understand your message. If you must use technical language, define your terms if even one member of your audience may not be able to follow.

Be consistent

Consistency means using the same term again rather than trying to come up with a synonym. For example, if you refer to your marketing plan at the beginning of the document, use the same term throughout. This book refers to communication skills throughout, not communicating talents or communication abilities. The same is true of the structure. Stay with your original pattern. If you structure part one I, A and 1, then part two should be II, A and 1, not 1.0, 2.1 and 3.5. Consistency makes it easier to follow.

Be specific

Being specific means being precise. You may say, for instance, that people perceived product XYZ in a certain way. However, it is clearer, more convincing and more accurate to say that five out of ten, or 50 per cent, of the people you sampled perceived the product in a particular way. When you discuss the fact that prices or costs have risen, be specific. Indicate by how much or by what percentage. Prices increased 50 per cent. Costs rose by 14 per cent. If it rained heavily, say that it rained 5 inches in two hours. Being specific will make your communication more credible.

Use appropriate images: verbal or non-verbal

People remember pictures and images. Therefore, it is important to use the best illustration, graph, blueprint or photograph available. It is also important to use verbal descriptions, examples or analogies to illustrate your points. If you want to explain a complex process, the audience may understand more easily if you are able to compare it to a more familiar example. Was the speed that of Concorde, or the number 52 bus? Did the amount of wasted paper in your company compare to a snowfall in the Alps? Because most of us are familiar with public transport or sports, you can frequently select analogies from those fields to illustrate your points.

Consider confidentiality

Be careful that you have not said or written anything that violates company policy. Because you are close to a project it is easy for you to talk comfortably about your involvement, but you need to think about your audience. You may inadvertently include some information in your communication that would not be appropriate for everyone to read or hear. Personnel issues or plans for new products are two areas that might be sensitive.

Be sensitive to inadvertent insults

None of us intends to insult, patronise or demean our audiences, but unless you read through your notes or reports carefully, you may do so unwittingly. Avoid referring to the opposite sex or to people in a certain age group – young or old – in a disparaging way. Be careful about your assumptions.

Summary

Having organised your thoughts and analysed your audience, it is important that you carefully select the right words, actions and images for the occasion. When you do:

- Avoid hyperbole
- Avoid qualifiers
- Keep your communication simple
- Be consistent
- Be specific
- Use appropriate images: verbal or non-verbal
- Consider confidentiality
- Be sensitive to inadvertent insults.

Thus far you have been very thoughtful, but there are still a few more points with which to concern yourself.

12

PAY ATTENTION TO DETAILS

You have been working on clarifying the message for the audience. You have thought about the organisation. You have sequenced information to enable the audience to follow your logic. You have thought about your word, image or gesture choices. You are about to send the message. As you know, once it is out of your hands or mouth, then someone else has control. It is essential that you take a moment to check and double check that your message is precisely the way you want it. The following are key areas where errors may occur.

Grammar and typography

Reread more than once. Put your work through your computer's grammar or spell check, and check it yourself too. How many times have you seen 'it's' when the author meant 'its', or vice versa? Often, you see a year or date that is wrong, for example a list of dates in a particular decade beginning with 18– instead of 19–. Perhaps on a reread you may notice that you have written a singular noun with a plural verb. We all make these errors; we simply have to remember to check for them.

Protocol and courtesy

You have seen people's names and titles misspelled or misused in a distribution list. You may also have seen a name omitted or put in the wrong order. Although this may sound a bit outmoded, people are often offended when they have worked hard for certain titles and then discover that they're missing from a letterhead or a report. You may pay a price for causing that offence. If the audience is annoyed with you they may be biased against what you are communicating. If there is no company policy about titles, be sure that there is a consistent one coming from your office, or from your department. Maybe in each other's offices you refer to a colleague by a nickname, but that nickname may not be appropriate when new clients are being pursued or you are meeting with your shareholders. What matters is that you have checked for details.

Accuracy and promises

Accuracy and promises go beyond spelling and grammar. Accuracy means being sure that your data is factually correct. If you have findings to substantiate your recommendations, they should be accurate. You need to check your maths. Is what you are saying true or is what you are saying something that you would *like* to be true?

Promises are agreements you have made in writing or verbally. It is vital that you keep any promises you have made. If a client has asked you to do a particular kind of research, it is important that you do what was asked. If you promised to return a call, send a message, or get back to someone, be sure that you do.

Balance

When you have thought through whatever it is that you want to communicate, think it through again. Read it through again. Be sure that you haven't spent ten minutes talking about point one and a total of five minutes on points two and three. Have you spent 20 pages preparing for argument number one, but only one page on number two? Is the entire document 60 pages in length, but your closing comments only two sentences? Ask yourself if your communication is balanced. Assuming that you have more than one point to make, look at the relative weight you give to each item in your communication.

Format and layout

What does the image look like? What does the report look like? Is your memo coffee- or tea-stained? Is your speech dog-eared? Are the notes you are using so yellowed with age that the audience will think you haven't updated the material in years? Is there adequate white space, so the document is easy to read? Are your visuals clear and simple? Is what you are presenting confusing because it is filled with too many type styles? With the advent of computers it is tempting to play with images and type faces, which can lead to clutter. Are the headings consistent in your chapters? Are all letters from your office typed a certain way?

Equipment

Double and triple check any mechanical, electrical or electronic equipment. Such items tend to have minds of their own. You certainly don't need a whiteboard with markers that have dried out or are too fine for the room size. You don't need overhead projectors with broken switches, finger smeared slides or burned out bulbs. Nor do you need a sensitive computer to crash when you need it. Is your VCR set to the right channel? Do the remote controls work? Is the flip chart on its last legs? Are you one chair short in the room? Did someone come without paper? Do you have enough copies of your handouts? Is there a microphone, and is it working? How tall is the lectern? Is the photocopier filled with paper or toner? Is there paper in your fax machine?

Summary

Pay attention to detail. Even when you think you have taken care of everything, you should check again to be sure that everything is in is in order. Be sure to check:

- Grammar and typography
- Protocol and courtesy
- Accuracy and promises
- Balance
- Format and layout
- Equipment

You should check not only the details in the message itself, but also the details about the sender – yourself.

13

LOOK AT YOURSELF

We have spent a good deal of time looking at words, visuals and graphics, but communication is also about images. One of the most important images that you communicate is your own. Effective communicators know what they project as individuals. Think about first impressions, because people really do take them into account. People notice what we wear, what we sound like, what our offices look like and how our staff presents itself. Do your own inventory and ask yourself more questions.

How do you look?

Take a good look in the mirror. Decide if you like your appearance. Think about what your personal style says about you. Think about your hair and your choice of clothing. Are you well-groomed and dressed appropriately for the situation? Have you chosen the most appropriate colours for you and for the occasion? Does your clothing detract from what you are communicating? For some, even an unpolished pair of shoes can be a distraction.

In addition to your choice of clothing, think about what you *do* with those clothes? Do you pull at a hem? Are you pushing your glasses up to the bridge of your nose? Are you running your hands through your hair? Are you twisting buttons? Are you fiddling with your tie or jamming your hands into your pockets? There is nothing wrong with any of these gestures, until they become distracting for the audience.

What about your posture or stance? Do you pace? Do you dance? Do you go up and down on your toes? Are your eyes glued down at your desk or gazing out of a window when you should be listening or watching others? Are you hunched up? Again, there is nothing wrong with any of these movements. Just know yourself.

How do you sound?

Are you easily understood? Do you have pet habits like clearing your throat before you speak. Do you 'um' and 'er' a lot? Do you have pet phrases? Is everything that you like 'marvellous'? Are you so predictable that people do not believe what you are saying? If everything is marvellous, then your audience may begin to wonder if you're hiding something.

Have you ever recorded your voice? Have you ever noticed if you have peculiar speech habits or idiosyncrasies? Do you have a strong, booming voice that might intimidate when you want to be lighthearted, or a soft, gentle voice that might sound passive when you want to assert yourself?

How does your office look?

Like your choice of clothing, your office reflects your personality. Cluttered or neat, your office projects your standards. You have to decide what image you want to project. Is your office filled with old dirty coffee cups? Is the wastepaper basket always full? Are there unopened letters and piles of messages that make you look sloppy or careless?

How do your colleagues look and sound?

Have you ever made a phone call to a company and heard the receptionist chewing gum over the phone in the middle of a conversation? Of course you have. In your company? Have you ever walked into a store only to discover that you have to interrupt a personal conversation in order to be served? Have you ever been greeted by a cold, unfriendly person, too busy to acknowledge your presence? In the reception area, are magazines, newspapers and journals months old? Conversely, have you been greeted with warmth and kindness? Have you been spoken to as if you mattered? The people who work for you reflect your standards.

Summary

When you check for details, don't forget to do your own inventory. Your image sends a message as well. Therefore, look at yourself and ask:

- How do I look?
- How do I sound?
- How does my office look?
- How do my colleagues look and sound?

You have done your homework: your messages are carefully thought through and effectively distributed. Now it is time to find out how you are doing, to get some feedback.

14

SEEK FEEDBACK: NEGATIVE AND POSITIVE

This is one of the best ways to boost your communication skills. You want to know whether or not your message has reached the audience as you intended. If it did, you want to know why so that you can do it again. If it did not, you want to know why not so that you can modify what you did. If you were the boss of all those people you met in the early pages of the book, it would be crucial for you and for your company to know why communication failed, and to ensure that it never failed again.

Feedback can be formal or informal. After a major presentation or submitting a major study you can ask for formal feedback. You can ask someone to write a critique of your communication. That is a useful exercise if the situation warrants it. But much communication is short and informal, and written feedback may be disproportionately time-consuming. Therefore, on a day-to-day basis you need

to seek feedback less formally. Consider these three suggestions for getting informal feedback: **listen**, **concentrate**
and **ask questions**.

Listen

What you want to know is:

- Whether or not your audience received the message;
- How people interpreted what you communicated;
- Why the audience did or did not understand what you
  communicated.

People volunteer that sort of information all the time. The
comments that you read in the first chapter of this book
are indicative of the kinds of informal feedback available.
Listen to what people say about what you and others have
communicated. Seek out feedback.

Unfortunately, listening is one of our weaker skills. As
we said, it's hard to concentrate when deadlines and other
pressures weigh heavily. It is easy to allow our minds to
wander when someone else is talking and no wonder; our
minds work extraordinarily quickly. We process information faster than anyone can speak, so there is plenty of
opportunity for our minds to roam.

Concentrate

We have to discipline ourselves, to catch ourselves as our
minds start to wander and refocus on the moment at hand.
How many times have you been reading a report or a memo
and realised that you can't remember what you just read?
How many times have you realised that you are not
focused? You have to go back and reread the preceding
passage or page. How often have you been talking to
someone and realised that you weren't really listening?

You attempt to capture the essence of what is being said by listening harder to the remaining part of the communication, or you ask to have something repeated.

Many people deliberately take notes when they are reading, on the phone or in a meeting. The purpose of the note-taking is not only to have a record of what transpired but also to help you concentrate on what is taking place.

What techniques do you use to help you concentrate on the communication that is occurring around you?

Ask questions

Asking questions is the most assertive way of getting the information that you want. Often, you need to probe. A question like, 'What did you think of the report?' may result only in a vague response: 'It was fine'; 'It was comprehensive'; 'It was persuasive'. Those are nice compliments, of course, but you want to know specifically why it was fine, comprehensive or persuasive. You want to know what you did right. You want to know what you need to work on in the future. To improve your skills it is essential that you are not too sensitive about negative feedback. As long as it is specific, you can work on the aspect of what you did that was less than excellent.

Summary

To determine whether or not your message has been conveyed it is important to seek out feedback. Basically, you want to improve when you have failed and you want to repeat the same technique when you have succeeded. Therefore, feedback, both negative and positive, is vital in boosting your communication skills. To obtain feedback:

- Listen   ■ Concentrate   ■ Ask questions

15

SEEK OPPORTUNITIES TO DEVELOP

The best way to develop your communication skills is to consciously seek opportunities to use your talents: to practise. And don't forget, developing your communication skills is a lifelong process.

Learn from what you do

You write. You read what you have written, and you rewrite. Perhaps you don't look at a report for a month once it is completed. Pick it up months or years later, read it and see if it still is clear to you. If it is, ask yourself what you did correctly. You want to be able to replicate the techniques you applied. If, on the other hand, you reread what you wrote and find it bewildering, analyse what you have done wrong and ask yourself why the memo or report is no longer clear. Learn from what you did.

Analysis is equally important when you are speaking. Replay the conversation or talk in your mind, but this time try to remember the reactions of the audience. Can you visualise when they were becoming fatigued or bored? Can you visualise when they clearly appeared to be following you? Can you recall when the bulk of the questions came? About what? Did the questions occur because you inspired them or because the audience was seeking clarity on what you had already said? Think about it. You are constantly trying to improve your talents.

You rewrite, you speak, you replay, you revise, you refine. You seek feedback, you get feedback, you learn from feedback.

Learn from what other people do

You see other people making presentations.. You read other people's work. You go to meetings. You read reports. You watch television. You set up interviews. You are interviewed. You attend press conferences. Every time you are exposed to someone else's communication it is an opportunity to apply your own critical eye or ear to what you are experiencing. If you attend meetings and hear superb speakers, analyse what they did in order to command attention and get their points across. If you read a report that is particularly well written, analyse it and determine what it was about the topic or the structure or the word choices or format that made it so easy to read.

Learn from what other people say

At the beginning of this book we listed comments made by Jim and his colleagues. Each of these comments represented a communication failure; but equally, each of them is feedback and provides you with an opportunity to make changes, share the information or assist someone else.

Welcome the information and take it on board whether it comes from a best friend, a colleague, a stranger or a supervisor.

55713

Apply what you have learned

When you see a technique or an approach that works and that you like, try it. Modify the ideas so that they work for your style. If someone used a mnemonic or wider margins or more graphs or fewer words and if they appeared to assist the audience in understanding, experiment with those strategies yourself.

Never hesitate to borrow successful communication techniques and adopt them to your own style and needs.

Practise

Look for opportunities to write reports. Look for opportunities to give the talk, to run meetings, to meet or hear new people. Speaking in public is frightening. A blank page can be equally threatening. But the more you write, the more you speak, the more you learn, if you are willing to assess your performance honestly.

Summary

Seek opportunities to develop. Developing your communication skills is a lifelong process:

■ Learn from what you do
■ Learn from what other people do
■ Apply what you have learned
■ Practise.